LATINO LIFE

HOLIDAYS AND CELEBRATIONS

Latino Life

Holidays and Celebrations

by Ruth Goring

Rourke Publications, Inc.

The following sources are acknowledged and thanked for the use of their photographs in this work: Bob Daemmrich pp. 2, 22, 33, 35, 38; James L. Shaffer pp. 7, 11; Lois Ellen Frank p. 9; Mark Nohl/New Mexico Economic Development and Tourism p. 12; Frances M. Roberts pp. 15, 23, 29, 37; Diane C. Lyell pp. 17, 19; Richard B. Levine pp. 18, 42; Robert Fried p. 25; AP/Wide World Photos p. 26; Martin Hutner p. 40.

Produced by Salem Press, Inc.

Copyright © 1995, by Rourke Publications, Inc.

All rights in this book are reserved. No part of this work may be used or reproduced in any manner whatsoever or transmitted in any form or by any means, electronic or mechanical, including photocopy, recording, or any information storage and retrieval system, without written permission from the copyright owner except in the case of brief quotations embodied in critical articles and reviews. For information address the publisher, Rourke Publications, Inc., P.O. Box 3328, Vero Beach, Florida 32964.

∞ The paper used in these volumes conforms to the American National Standard for Permanence of Paper for Printed Library Materials, Z39.48-1984.

Library of Congress Cataloging-in-Publication Data

Goring, Ruth, 1954-
  Holidays and celebrations / by Ruth Goring.
     p.   cm. — (Latino life)
  ISBN 0-86625-542-7
  1. Hispanic Americans—Folklore. 2. Festivals—United States—Juvenile literature. 3. Holidays—United States—Juvenile literature. 4. Festivals—Latin America—Juvenile literature. 5. Holidays—Latin America—Juvenile literature. 6. United States—Social life and customs—Juvenile literature. 7. Latin America—Social life and customs—Juvenile literature. [1. Hispanic Americans—Social life and customs. 2. Holidays. 3. Festivals.] I. Title. II. Series.
GR111.H57G67   1995
394.2'6'08968073—dc20   94-49568
                                                                                             CIP
                                                                                             AC

First Printing

PRINTED IN THE UNITED STATES OF AMERICA

Contents

Chapter 1	Family Celebrations		6
Chapter 2	Religious Holidays		13
Chapter 3	Patriotic Holidays		21
Chapter 4	Folk Festivals		32
	Calendar of Latino Holidays and Celebrations		43
	Glossary		45
	More About Latino Holidays and Celebrations		46
	Index		47

Chapter 1

Family Celebrations

Fiesta! Many people who have never learned Spanish know that that word means "party." Spanish-speaking Americans (often called Latinos or Hispanic Americans) like to celebrate. They enjoy putting on parties.

Latinos celebrate for many reasons. Sometimes they gather to celebrate a religious holiday. Parades, special programs, and parties help them remember the history of their country of origin. Some Latinos hold festivals to enjoy the music, dances, costumes, and foods of their heritage. Some *fiestas* are more private, celebrating someone's birthday, First Communion, or wedding.

When Latinos are asked what is most important to them, most will answer, "My family." To learn about Latino *fiestas,* then, it helps to start with celebrations in the family.

Baptism

Most Latinos in the United States are Roman Catholic. Centuries ago, Spanish explorers who set up colonies in Central and South America brought Catholic priests with them. Later, the colonies gained their independence from Spain. Some of the new governments made special agreements with the Catholic church. Often the church was given the responsibility of running schools for all the country's children.

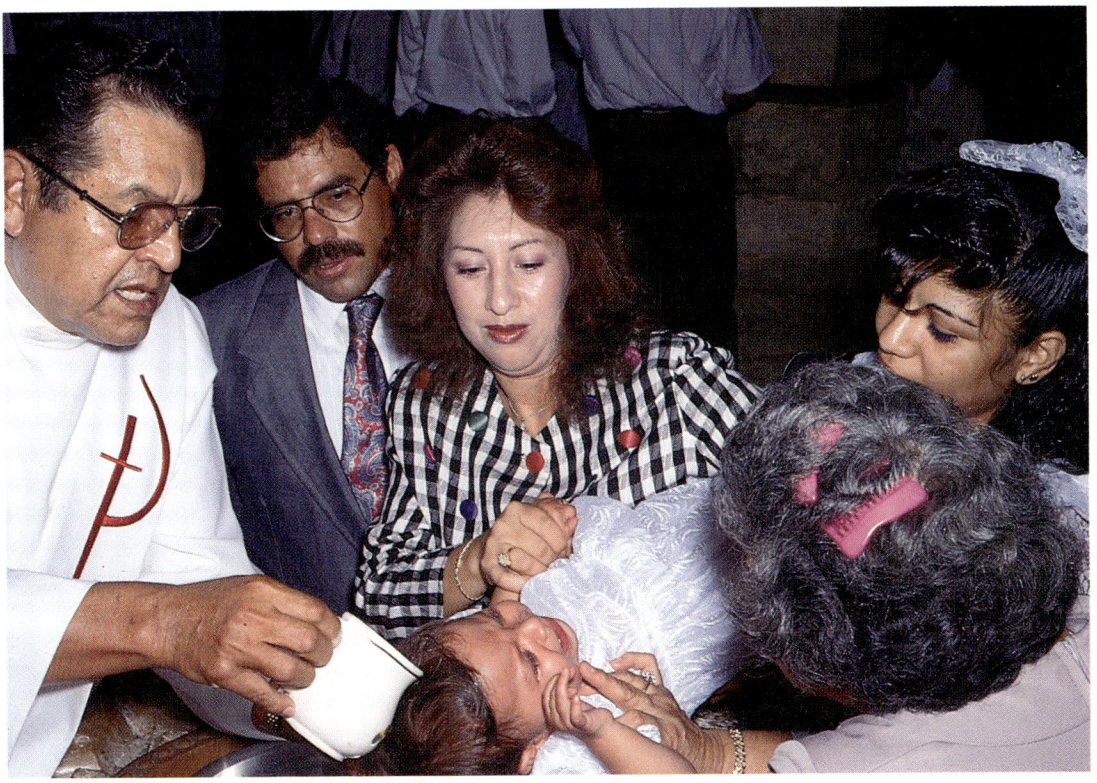

Parents and godparents watch as the priest baptizes a baby.

It is not surprising, then, that many Latino parents in the United States want to bring up their children as Roman Catholics. In neighborhoods where there are lots of Latinos, churches may offer services in Spanish and in English.

Catholics welcome a newborn child into the world—and into the church—with baptism. The parents bring the baby to a special Mass at church. The baby is dressed in fine clothes. There is a special time for the parents to take the baby to the front of the sanctuary. The child's godparents, called *padrinos,* join in the baptism. They promise to help care for the little one and teach him or her about God. The priest puts some water on the child's head. Next, he says a prayer for the baby and announces the child's name. Everyone is glad that the family and the church have a new member. Afterward, the parents and godparents may hold a party at home. They celebrate the baptism with music and good food.

Some Latinos have left the Catholic church and have joined evangelical or Pentecostal churches. Most of these churches also practice baptism, but its meaning is different. For them, baptism shows that a person has decided to accept the Christian faith. These churches usually do not baptize small children, who cannot make that decision for themselves. Baptism for teenagers or adults in these churches may be a quiet ceremony. Other times it may come with lots of singing and clapping. The people may have dinner together afterward to continue the celebration.

First Communion

One of the most important events in a Catholic child's life is First Communion. Usually, it happens when the child is six or seven years old. For months beforehand, groups of children gather in classes at school or church. They learn about Christian faith and talk about what the Communion, or Eucharist, means. They practice for the ceremony that allows them to take part in their first Communion.

When the big day arrives, the children's *padrinos* are there to join the celebration. The boys wear ties and white shirts; the girls are bright in their long white dresses and veils. They may carry candles as they enter the church. First, there is a program of music and prayer. Next, each girl or boy walks to the altar to receive a communion wafer. This wafer is a thin, flat circle of bread with no yeast. The bread has a special meaning. It reminds Christians that Jesus gave up his life on the cross.

The celebration does not end with this ceremony. There is nearly always a party or picnic afterward. The children who have celebrated Communion often receive presents from their friends and family.

Birthdays and Saints' Days

Many Latino families celebrate birthdays with a cake and presents. Other parts of their birthday celebrations reflect their cultural heritage. Many of the guests may speak Spanish, and they probably enjoy *salsa* or *merengue* music. The food is also different. Mexican families enjoy *tamales*, or meat wrapped in cornmeal and cornhusks. Dominican and Puerto Rican families celebrate with small meat pies known as *pasteles*. Colombian families may fix sancocho, a soup made with plantains (a type of banana), and round cornbreads known as *arepas*.

A birthday party for Mexican and other Latino children often includes a *piñata* as well. The piñata is formed around a clay pot or papier-mâché container. Most piñatas are made in the shape of an animal. They are decorated with bright-colored tissue paper and foil. An adult hangs the piñata on a rope or cord over a tree branch. Sometimes, the piñata is hung inside from the ceiling. One person keeps hold of the end of the rope.

Bright-colored tissue paper decorates the outside of this festive piñata.

Beginning with the youngest, the children take turns putting on a blindfold. Then, they beat the air with a stick, hoping to hit the piñata and break it. Meanwhile, the person holding the rope is raising and lowering the piñata. Moving the piñata makes it even harder to find. Sooner or later, someone does give it a hard whack and brings it down. When it breaks, candies spill out and all the children scramble to get their share.

Some Latino families name their children for Catholic saints, people who lived long ago who were very close to God. Each saint is honored on a certain day of the year. When a child's saint's day comes, the family may celebrate with a special meal. For the child, it is almost like having an extra birthday.

THE QUINCEAÑERA

For Latina girls, one birthday party is bigger than all the rest: the fifteenth. This event is called the *quinceañera*. This age is when a girl becomes a young woman and leaves her childhood behind. For Catholic girls, it is also a time to renew religious promises.

Months of planning go into the quinceañera. The family must decide when should it be held. Sometimes the party happens weeks after the girl's actual birthday so out-of-town relatives can come. The girl and her family decide who her attendants will be. She chooses a boy as her escort for the day. She may invite fourteen other boys (called *chambelanes*) and fourteen girls (called *damas*) to be part of her "court." Next, the family decides where to hold the celebration. Part of the celebration is a special Mass, held in the church. The party afterward may take place in a home, a hotel, or a community center.

When the day comes, the attendants lead the way into the church. It is like a wedding, since the girls wear fancy dresses and the boys wear tuxedos. The honored girl, wearing a long dress and carrying a bouquet, follows them. Her parents join her. Her *padrinos* are there too, ready to

A young Latina reads her vows during her quinceañera Mass.

show their support. The girl stands with her parents at the front of the church, with her attendants nearby.

Part of the ceremony is a quinceañera Mass. During the Mass, the girl shows that she is ready to keep her promises to God and to the church. Now she will keep these promises as an adult rather than as a child. She may take a flower from her bouquet and place it at the shrine of a saint. Usually, this saint is one that is important to her family. When the priest serves the Eucharist, she is the first to receive the communion wafer.

That evening, people of all ages come to the *fiesta de quinceañera* (fifteen-year-old's party). The room is decorated with balloons and flowers. There is plenty of food and a beautiful cake. The musicians get their instruments ready.

The girl's court attendants walk onto the dance floor, forming two rows. The girl and her escort pass between them. After the girl sits in a seat of honor, her father removes her flat-heeled shoes. He puts shiny new high heels on her feet. The father and daughter dance the first dance together. Then, the girl's escort takes over as her dance partner.

The dancing, eating, and celebrating may continue late into the night. The girl will never forget this day—the day when she left childhood behind and became a young woman.

Chapter 2

RELIGIOUS HOLIDAYS

For most Latinos, religious holidays are an important part of family and community life. Even if a Latino family does not attend church regularly, they join in these celebrations. They enjoy the special parties, parades, and festivals that celebrate saints' days and religious events.

NAVIDAD (CHRISTMAS)

Christmas is one of the high points of the year for Latinos. December 25 is a time when all Christians celebrate the birth of Jesus Christ. Many Catholic Latino groups begin their parties in mid-December with Las Posadas. In Las Posadas, a group of people act out a Bible story. They pretend they are Mary and Joseph, the parents of Jesus. As the group walks along, they pretend to look for an inn where they might spend the night. They also sing and carry candles and small figures of Mary and Joseph. The people stop at their friends' houses and ask for lodging. At first, all the friends say no. Finally, one family opens its door and gives a happy welcome. Everyone gathers inside for a piñata, *pan dulce* (sweet bread), hot chocolate, and more singing.

Some communities celebrate Las Posadas for nine days, December 16-24. In other cities, it is a larger celebration held on just one day. San Antonio, Texas, for example, holds Las Posadas each year on the second Sunday in December. Musicians and children dressed as Mary,

Some churches reenact the story of Las Posadas during the Christmas season.

Joseph, shepherds, and angels walk down a street called the Paseo del Río. The Spanish word *río* means river. As its name shows, this street runs along a river. The walk ends at the Plaza Juárez, where the celebration includes folk dancing, music, and a piñata party.

Latino families of other Christian faiths celebrate Christmas with carol singing and pageants in December. The highlight of the celebration comes on Christmas Eve and Christmas Day. This is the time when family members exchange gifts and church members gather to worship and eat together.

For Catholic Latinos, *Nochebuena* (Christmas Eve) and *Navidad* (Christmas Day) are also important. On the day of Christmas Eve, some people take their pets to church for a "blessing of the animals." This event honors the animals that attended Jesus' birth in a stable. In the evening, families usually get together for a meal. Among Puerto Ricans, this dinner includes rice, beans, pork, and meat pies called *pasteles*. Cuban Americans also like to eat pork, and they finish this meal with *turrones* (special candies from Spain). Many people go to Mass later that night. Some Latinos call this mass *la misa del gallo* (the Rooster Mass) because it begins at midnight and ends early in the morning, when roosters crow.

Most Catholic Latinos have adopted the North American custom of opening gifts on Christmas Day. Others still celebrate the traditional way, with the twelve days of Christmas that end on January 6. This day is known as Día de los Tres Reyes Magos (Day of the Three Kings). It honors the Bible story of the Three Wise Men (Magi) who came to worship the baby Jesus. On the night of January 5, children put a shoe outside the door. They may stuff the shoe with straw or put out a bowl of water. The straw and water are left for the wise men's camels. In the morning, they run to look at their shoes. They find the straw and water gone and the shoes full of candy and gifts.

Later that day, there is a big dinner. The meal ends with a special dessert—the Three Kings Cake. This cake is

A costumed wise man offers a gift to a small angel at a parade held on the Day of the Three Kings.

baked in the shape of a crown. It is decorated with bits of candied pineapple and cherries to look like jewels. Often a small prize—a ring or a doll—is baked into it. People are eager to find the prize in their piece of cake. The one who finds the prize is supposed to have good luck for the year.

SEMANA SANTA (HOLY WEEK)

The week before Easter is called Semana Santa, or Holy Week. Latinos of many Christian faiths attend special church services during this time. They remember Jesus' death on a cross and honor his rising to new life. The celebrations begin on Palm Sunday. On that day, children march through the church waving palm branches. They are acting out a Bible story. In this story, Jesus came into Jerusalem not long before he died. When they saw Jesus, crowds of people waved palm branches and called Jesus their king.

On the Thursday after Palm Sunday, people attend special church services. They remember Jesus' last gathering with the twelve men who had been closest to him. This gathering is known as the Last Supper. The next day is Good Friday, when the story is told of how Jesus was nailed to a cross. This is a very serious day. Many Catholic churches are left dark, and black cloth is draped over the cross and the altar.

Easter Sunday is a happy day. People go to church again. This time, they find the sanctuary full of light and music. The priest or pastor announces, "Christ has risen!" After church, people go home to a big family dinner. Some Latino children have Easter egg hunts in the afternoon. They play with *cascarones,* whole eggshells filled with bits of colored paper. They enjoy tossing the cascarones at each other. They like to crack the shells on people's heads so the confetti falls out like colored snow.

DÍA DE LOS MUERTOS (DAY OF THE DEAD)

Día de los Muertos is a holiday celebrated in Mexico. It is celebrated in many Mexican American communities in

A young girl dips her cascarón, *or confetti egg, into colored dye.*

A family makes their offerings before an altar decorated in honor of Día de los Muertos.

the United States as well. It falls on November 2, also known as All Souls Day. This is a day for families to honor relatives who have died. They may pull weeds from the graves and decorate the graves with flowers and small statues. Instead of only feeling sad because the relatives are dead, family members often bring a picnic to the cemetery. They may even sing, dance, and tell stories. Bakeries make special *panes de muertos*—"death breads" shaped like humans or animals. Some Catholic churches hold a Mass to encourage people to pray for those who have died.

Patron Saints' Days

Many Latino Catholics hold annual celebrations to honor "patron saints." These saints are holy persons who lived long ago. Many Catholics believe these saints spend their time in Heaven watching over certain groups of people. The patron saint of Mexico is Our Lady of Guadalupe. A legend says that a vision of Mary appeared to an Indian named

Juan Diego in 1531. He saw her on a hill near Mexico City. She told Juan to go to a dry hillside. When he obeyed, he found beautiful roses blooming there. Then she sent him to speak to the bishop. When Juan opened his *serape* (cloak) to show the roses to the bishop, the roses disappeared. In their place, a picture of Mary appeared.

The day of Our Lady of Guadalupe is December 12, but the celebration may last for several days. In Las Cruces, New Mexico, people climb a mountain carrying candles and roses to honor Mary. Later in the day, they perform Hispanic and Indian dances. Everyone celebrates with a big dinner. Many other Mexican American communities have similar celebrations.

An important day for Puerto Ricans is June 24. This is the day of Saint John the Baptist. San Juan, Puerto Rico's

An altar dedicated to the Virgin of Guadalupe.

capital, is named for this saint. One celebration is held at the Newport Beach Resort in Sunny Isles, near Miami, Florida. This celebration is known as Celebración San Juan and lasts for three days. Puerto Ricans gather to enjoy merengue music, traditional foods, arts, crafts, costumes, and dancing. Celebrations of John the Baptist's day are usually held near the sea. At midnight, people are supposed to go into the water as if they were being baptized.

Cuban American children learn the story of Mary's appearance many years ago in Santiago, Cuba. This vision of Mary is called Our Lady of Charity, and she is the patron saint of Cuba. On her day, September 8, Cuban Americans in Miami and other cities get together for parades and parties. At Mass, they light candles and set out flowers to honor Our Lady of Charity.

Latinos also celebrate and remember many other saints' days and holy days. These days include the Virgin of Candelaria (February 2), Saint Joseph (March 19), the Holy Cross (May 3), Corpus Christi (early June), Our Lady of Monserratt (September 8), and Saint Francis (October 4).

Chapter 3

PATRIOTIC HOLIDAYS

Many Latinos like to celebrate two sets of patriotic holidays. They celebrate the patriotic holidays of their adopted country, the United States. They also celebrate special holidays of the country they (or their relatives) came from. On these patriotic days, many Latino parents and teachers tell the children about their country of origin. Many Latino communities also organize parades and festivals to show that they are proud of their heritage. This chapter will tell about the history of a few patriotic holidays celebrated by Latinos.

SEPTEMBER 15-16 (MEXICO AND CENTRAL AMERICA)

Dieciséis is a Spanish word that means "sixteen." It also is the name Mexicans give to September 16—a very important date in Mexican history. For centuries, beginning in the 1500's, Spain ruled over many lands outside its border in Europe. It ruled most of South America, Central America, and western North America. Mexico and Central America were then called New Spain.

In the early 1800's, some Mexican leaders were unhappy with Spanish rule. The Mexicans thought that the taxes they had to pay were too high. They complained that the Spanish trade laws were unfair. People of Spanish ancestry who were born in New Spain were especially unhappy. These people

Two Latina girls carry a banner in a Dieciséis parade celebrating Mexican independence.

were known as *criollos*. They did not like the *peninsulares*—the people who had come from Spain to carry out the government's wishes. Some criollos started talking secretly about trying to win independence for New Spain.

One leader among the criollos was Father Miguel Hidalgo, a priest in a small town called Dolores. He was part of a group that began plotting to get rid of Spanish rule. They hoped to start the revolution on October 1, 1810. In September, a spy told the Spanish viceroy, or governor, about the plan. When the rebels learned that someone had betrayed their plot, they sent a messenger to warn Father Hidalgo.

The messenger galloped into Dolores while it was still dark on Sunday morning, September 16, 1810. He awoke the priest and gave him the bad news. Father Hidalgo decided there was no time to lose. While some men went to gather weapons, Father Hidalgo hurried to the church in the town's main plaza. He and a few other men rang the bell and called the townspeople together. Father Hidalgo then made a speech that became famous as "el Grito de Dolores" (the Cry of Dolores). He asked the people to stand up against Spain and fight for freedom and justice. He ended his speech by shouting, "Long live America! Long live religion! Down with bad government!" The people eagerly echoed his cheer.

Hidalgo led a ragtag army through several battles. Later, the Spanish captured him. He was executed on July 30, 1811. New Spain did not actually win its independence until 1821. Although Hidalgo did not take part in the final victory, Mexican people remember his courage. Each year around midnight between September 15 and 16, people reenact the Grito de Dolores in the great square in Mexico City.

Several other Central American countries celebrate September 15 as their Independence Day. These countries include Costa Rica, Guatemala, El Salvador, Nicaragua,

Two young girls from Guatemala wear traditional clothing in a parade celebrating Latino pride.

and Honduras. On September 15, 1821, leaders of these areas decided to split off from New Spain (Mexico), which had just won its independence from Spain.

Many Latinos whose heritage is Mexican, Guatemalan, Honduran, Salvadoran, or Nicaraguan get together to celebrate these independence days at the same time. They hold parties, parades, and special programs. Even though these areas are now separate nations, their people share a history of fighting for independence from Spain.

Cinco de Mayo (Mexico)

Another favorite patriotic holiday for Mexican Americans is Cinco de Mayo (May 5). On this day, they remember a surprising Mexican victory over foreign invaders in 1862. They honor the memory of one of Mexico's greatest national heroes—Benito Juárez.

Benito Juárez was a Zapotec Indian who became president of Mexico in 1861. Juárez had already helped to write a set of laws for the new Mexican government. These laws were called La Reforma (the Reform). Under these laws, people of all religions were given freedom to practice their faith. The government planned to take over the school system so all children could receive education. Some wealthy Mexicans did not like Juárez's reforms.

In 1861, the French emperor Napoleon III decided to invade Mexico because the Mexican government owed money to France. When the French forces arrived, conservative Mexicans welcomed them. Juárez's followers put up a fierce fight. They met the French soldiers in a battle at Puebla on May 5, 1862. The Mexican soldiers had poor weapons, but they fought bravely. Amazingly, the Mexicans succeeded in turning back the well-armed French forces.

Unfortunately, the French were not yet ready to leave Mexico. They won other victories, and in 1864 they drove Juárez out of Mexico City. Within a few years, though, the French soldiers gave up and returned home. When they left,

A young girl wears a traditional Mexican sombrero at a Cinco de Mayo festival.

Crowds line the streets at a Puerto Rican Independence Day parade in New York City.

Juárez returned to the presidency. When modern Mexican Americans celebrate Cinco de Mayo, they remember the courage of those who resisted the French invasion.

Día de la Raza (Puerto Rico, Dominican Republic, and Other Countries)

Christopher Columbus' landing in the New World on October 12, 1492, is a national holiday in the United States. This holiday has special meaning for many Latinos. Columbus' first landing was on the eastern side of an island that he called Hispaniola. Part of the island is now known as the Dominican Republic. The western third is the French-speaking country of Haiti. Dominican Americans, especially in New York City and New Jersey, take pride in celebrating Columbus' landing. For them and for other Latinos, October 12 is known as Día de la Raza or Día de la Hispanidad. It is a time for them to celebrate their Hispanic heritage. On this day, Latinos hold parades and festivals.

Puerto Ricans also make a holiday of November 19. On that day in 1493, Columbus arrived on the island that eventually was named Puerto Rico. Puerto Ricans call this day Discovery Day.

Birthday of José Martí (Cuba)

Christopher Columbus landed on the island of Cuba on October 27, 1492. About ten years later, Spain sent a governor and soldiers to take charge of the island. From the start, there was trouble between the Spanish and the Tainos, the native Indians who lived on the island. As more Spanish-speaking people and their slaves began to settle on the island, they also became unhappy with the way they were treated by the Spanish government.

The Spanish found out that the climate and soil of Cuba were just right for growing sugarcane and tobacco. They made settlers in Cuba plant these crops on large farms. By the 1830's, Cuba exported more sugar than any other country or colony in the world. Still, the Cuban people were not getting a fair share of the money from these crops.

A Cuban boy named José Martí began speaking out against the Spanish rulers. He was so bold that he was forced to leave the country when he was only sixteen years old. After that, he spent many years in Spain and in the United States. He wrote articles and books about politics in Latin America, and he also became a well-known poet.

Meanwhile, the Spanish finally ended slavery in Cuba in 1886. However, the Cubans were still unhappy, because the Spanish did not keep other promises they had made. Martí decided to return to Cuba with others who were ready to fight the Spanish.

Martí and his friends arrived in Cuba in May, 1895. Martí had never fought in a war before, and he did not even know how to ride a horse. On May 19, however, he got on horseback to lead a group of rebels against the Spanish. He died in battle that same day.

Cubans and Cuban Americans think of José Martí as their greatest national hero. His birthday, January 28, is one of their most important patriotic holidays.

INDEPENDENCE DAY (CUBA)

After José Martí died, the Cubans kept fighting for freedom from Spain. They knew that the money from sugar crops was very important to the Spanish. That is why the Cubans burned many sugarcane fields and destroyed sugar mills. They were determined to get the Spanish out of their land.

People in the United States worried about the fighting in Cuba. In 1898, President William McKinley sent a U.S. battleship, the *Maine*, to the harbor in Havana, Cuba. Americans who had been living in Cuba were taken on board. They believed they would be safe on an American ship, but they were wrong. On February 15, 1898, the *Maine* exploded, and 266 Americans were killed.

Now the United States was ready to enter the war. American troops came to Cuba to put an end to Spanish

A colorful dancer wears patriotic colors at a Cuban Day parade.

rule, and they succeeded. The war ended on August 12, 1898, when Spain surrendered. An American military government took over on January 1, 1899. Many Cuban Americans continue to honor January 1 as their independence day.

■ 29 ■

National Holidays of Latin American Countries

Argentina	May 25	Established its first independent government in 1810
Bolivia	August 6	Declared independence from Spain, Argentina, and Peru in 1825
Chile	September 18	First Chilean government elected in 1810
Colombia	July 20	Rebellion against Spanish rule in 1810
Costa Rica	September 15	Won independence from Spain and New Spain in 1821
Cuba	January 1	U.S. troops put an end to Spanish rule in 1899
Dominican Republic	February 27	Won independence from Haiti in 1844
	August 16	Regained independence after being occupied by Haiti
Ecuador	August 10	Rebellion against Spanish rule in 1809
El Salvador	September 15	Won independence from Spain and New Spain in 1821
Guatemala	September 15	Won independence from Spain and New Spain in 1821

Honduras	September 15	Won independence from Spain and New Spain in 1821
Mexico	September 16	Father Miguel Hidalgo y Costilla began Mexico's fight for independence from Spain in 1810
	May 5	Mexican villagers defeated a French invasion in 1862
Nicaragua	September 15	Won independence from Spain and New Spain in 1821
Panama	November 3	Declared independence from Colombia in 1903
Paraguay	May 14-15	Declared independence from Spain in 1811
Peru	July 28	Declared independence from Spain in 1821
Puerto Rico	November 19	Columbus landed in Puerto Rico in 1493
	September 24	Rebellion against Spanish rule in 1868
Uruguay	August 25	Declared independence from Brazil in 1825
Venezuela	July 5	Declared independence from Spain in 1811

Chapter 4

Folk Festivals

Each year, towns and cities across the United States hold festivals to celebrate Latino history and tradition. If people had an entire year to travel anywhere in the United States, they could go from one city to another, enjoying Latino parades, costumes, food, and music.

Winter

From early February to the middle of March, the Carnaval Miami is held in Miami, Florida. The center of this festival is Calle Ocho, or Southwest Eighth Street, located in a part of Miami called Little Havana. Many Cuban Americans own shops and restaurants on this street. The residents of Calle Ocho help organize the largest street party in the United States during Carnaval Miami. About a million and a half visitors come to the festival each year. Visitors enjoy tasting lots of Latino food. They also can play games at carnival booths and buy arts and crafts. Musicians and other entertainers perform at the festival. People compete in a golf tournament, a cooking contest, a beauty contest, and a race. This is the place to go to enjoy Cuban food, music, and dances.

Around the same time of year, the Charro Days festival happens in Brownsville, Texas. It is held for four days in February or early March. The Spanish word *charro* means "loud" or "flashy." This word was used to describe the *rancheros*, or ranchers, who helped win Mexico's independence from Spain. The rancheros were known for

This Latina wears a ruffled white dress as she rides side-saddle during a **charreada** *parade.*

their fancy clothes. These clothes included large *sombreros* (wide-brimmed hats), jackets embroidered with silver thread, and big spurs on their boots. Latinos in Texas have celebrated Charro Days each year since the 1950's. The celebration began as a *charreada*, or Mexican rodeo. Now it includes parades, concerts, fireworks, dances, games, food booths, arts and crafts, and costume displays.

SPRING

Some Mexican Americans in East Los Angeles, California, enjoy an unusual festival each year around April 1. This celebration is known as the PochoFest. It pokes fun at certain Mexican Americans, known as the Pochos. The Pochos are people who act like they have forgotten their Mexican heritage. They cannot speak Spanish, they know little about Mexican customs, and hot peppers make them cough. People at the festival pick a festival queen and king each year. Once they are crowned, the queen and king lead the Pocho Parade. The marching Pochos act like clowns. People who line up to watch the parade throw tortilla chips and corn nuts at them.

Rock Springs, Wyoming, hosts a Hispanic Heritage Festival on the first Saturday after Easter. This festival is busy with games, arts and crafts, music, dances, contests, and special exhibits.

Each year during the last week of April, people who like Mexican music can travel to Tucson, Arizona. There, they can hear concerts by *mariachi* groups. *Mariachis* play Mexican folk music. Their instruments include the guitar, the *guitarrón* (a cross between a bass fiddle and a guitar), the *vihuela* (a small string instrument), the cornet, and the trumpet. The groups gather each year for the Tucson International Mariachi Conference. Visitors also can enjoy performances by folk-dance groups. Others spend time at the Garibaldi Fiesta in downtown Tucson. This fiesta has Mexican food, an art exhibit, crafts, games, and a parade.

An **orquesta** *plays for crowds at a festival near the San Jose Mission in San Antonio, Texas.*

The Tejano Conjunto Festival is held in mid-May each year in San Antonio, Texas. People attend the festival for five days to hear *conjunto* musicians perform their special kind of Mexican American music. The Spanish word *conjunto* means "musical group." Conjunto music began in northern Mexico and southern Texas in the late 1800's. Each conjunto uses accordions and twelve-string guitars along with other instruments. "Tejano" conjunto music is played in Texas. It is different from the "Norteño" conjunto music that is played in northern Mexico. The Tejano Conjunto Festival, which began in 1982, is held in Rosedale Park, Mission County Park, and Market Square. The musicians play day and night. Those who come to listen also can buy Mexican American food and arts and crafts. Children can play games at booths, and people of all ages can join in dances.

In 1989, the New Orleans Hispanic Heritage Foundation started the Carnaval Latino of New Orleans. This festival is held each year on a weekend in the middle of June. At first, the Carnaval Latino was in the French Quarter. When that area became too crowded, it was moved to City Park in Marconi Meadows in 1994. Each year, people at the festival elect a Carnaval Latino queen to lead a parade. Latino musicians and other entertainers also perform. Many of New Orleans' famous restaurants set up food booths.

Summer

The Latino World Festival brings many well-known Latino and Spanish musicians to Detroit, Michigan. The festival lasts for three days during the third week in July. It began in 1971 and has always been held in Hart Plaza in downtown Detroit. Booths offer ethnic food, and there are games for children. Visitors are invited to a Catholic Mass on Sunday morning.

Since 1970, the Hispanic American Festival has been held in late July in El Barrio. This neighborhood is a mostly Latino area of Washington, D.C. The celebration is also known as the Festival Latino. In the early years, this festival included only folk dances and Hispanic food. Several other events were added later, including soccer games, the crowning of a festival queen, and a fancy-dress ball. On the last Sunday in July, the festival stages a grand parade. There are also contests, music and dance performances, dramas, and food from many Latin American countries.

Another neighborhood celebration is the Festival del Barrio. This festival takes place during the last week of August in Philadelphia, Pennsylvania. It is held on North Fifth Street, where many Puerto Ricans live. They are the largest Hispanic group in Philadelphia. This festival has lots of Puerto Rican food, music, and costumes.

La Fiesta de las Flores, or Festival of the Flowers, happens Labor Day weekend each year in El Paso, Texas. The El Paso Chamber of Commerce helps organize the festival, which is held in Washington Park. The festival has

Glittering costumes are worn by the dancers in this Brazilian Fest parade celebrating carnaval season.

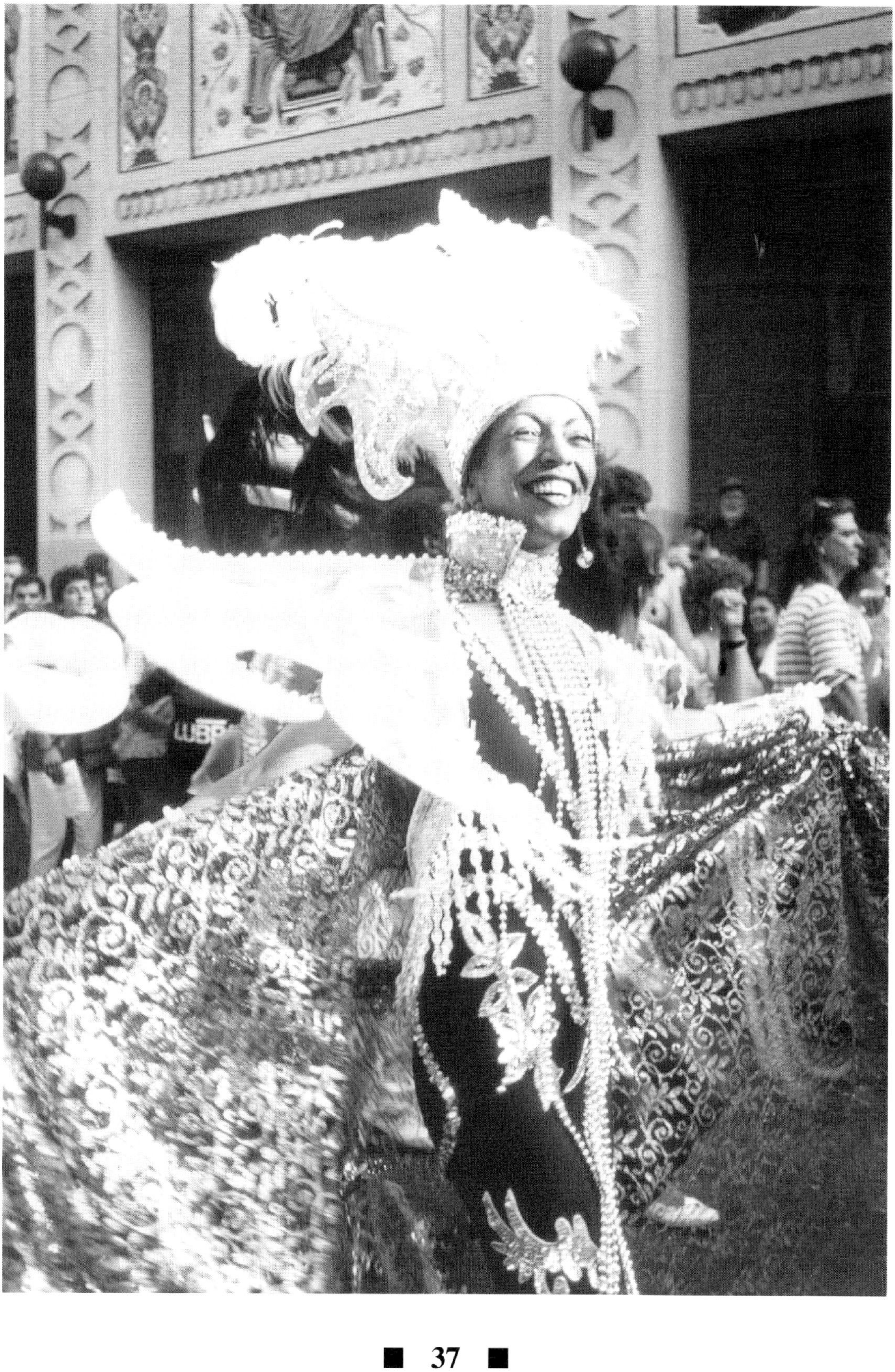

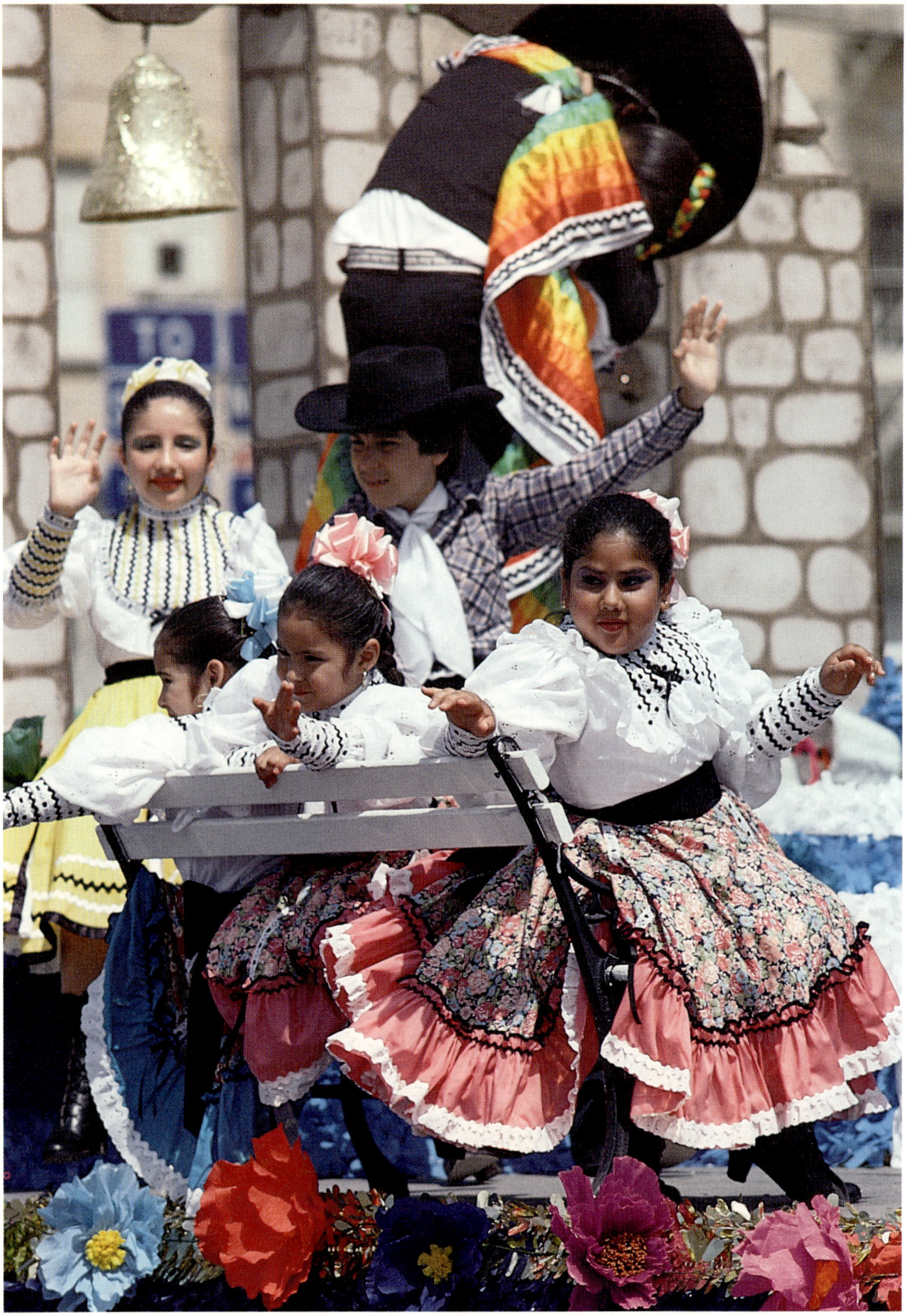

folk music, dance, games, arts and crafts, and costumes. More than half of the performers are Mexican or Mexican American.

AUTUMN

Each year, the president of the United States proclaims one week in September as Hispanic Heritage Week. This is a time to pay extra attention to Latinos. During this time, people learn how Latinos have made the United States a richer and more interesting place. In Washington, D.C., the celebrations will not all fit into one week. People there have decided to declare the whole month of September as Hispanic Heritage Month. Hispanic fashion designers put on a major fashion show, and there are concerts and lectures about Hispanic life. A group of Hispanic members of Congress and other political leaders sponsor the Hispanic Heritage Week Annual Dinner. Latinos who have had special success in business, education, or the arts receive awards at the dinner.

A Puerto Rican Week Festival is held in downtown Philadelphia during the last week of September. Many Puerto Rican music groups perform. Cuban American and other Latino musicians also perform. Each year, more than 100,000 visitors come to enjoy the music as well as food, dancing, games, and crafts.

Even more people gather at Bayfest in Corpus Christi, Texas, on the last weekend of September. Bayfest is a popular international festival held on North Shoreline Boulevard, near the Gulf of Mexico. Although it is not called a Hispanic celebration, more than half of its performers are Mexican American. The festival is held on a beach. It includes traditional dancing, music, foods, and games. People at the festival also enjoy raft races and a race for "anything-that-floats-but-a-boat." They can watch Coast Guard rescue demonstrations and a fireworks display over the bay.

The Border Folk Festival lasts for three to six days in

Bright paper flowers echo the rainbow colors of the costumes worn by these young Latino dancers.

early October. It has been held each year since 1973. The festival is held at the Chamizal National Memorial in El Paso, Texas. This is the place where a boundary dispute between the United States and Mexico was settled peacefully many years ago. The festival offers traditional food, arts, crafts, and special programs for children. There is lots of music and dance.

The whole month of October is set aside for the Hispanic Heritage Festival in Dade County, Florida. The festival is centered in Miami. Cuban Americans and other Latinos

Two Latinas wearing embroidered dresses and colorful hats attend a Peruvian festival held in Los Angeles.

display their folk arts and other crafts. Actors perform a play based on Christopher Columbus' voyage to the New World. Other special activities include a fancy ball, a golf tournament, and concerts at Tropical Park.

These are just some of the festivals where Americans can enjoy the food, music, dance, and art of Latinos. Since Latinos are the fastest-growing ethnic group in the United States, it is likely that Latino folk festivals will grow too.

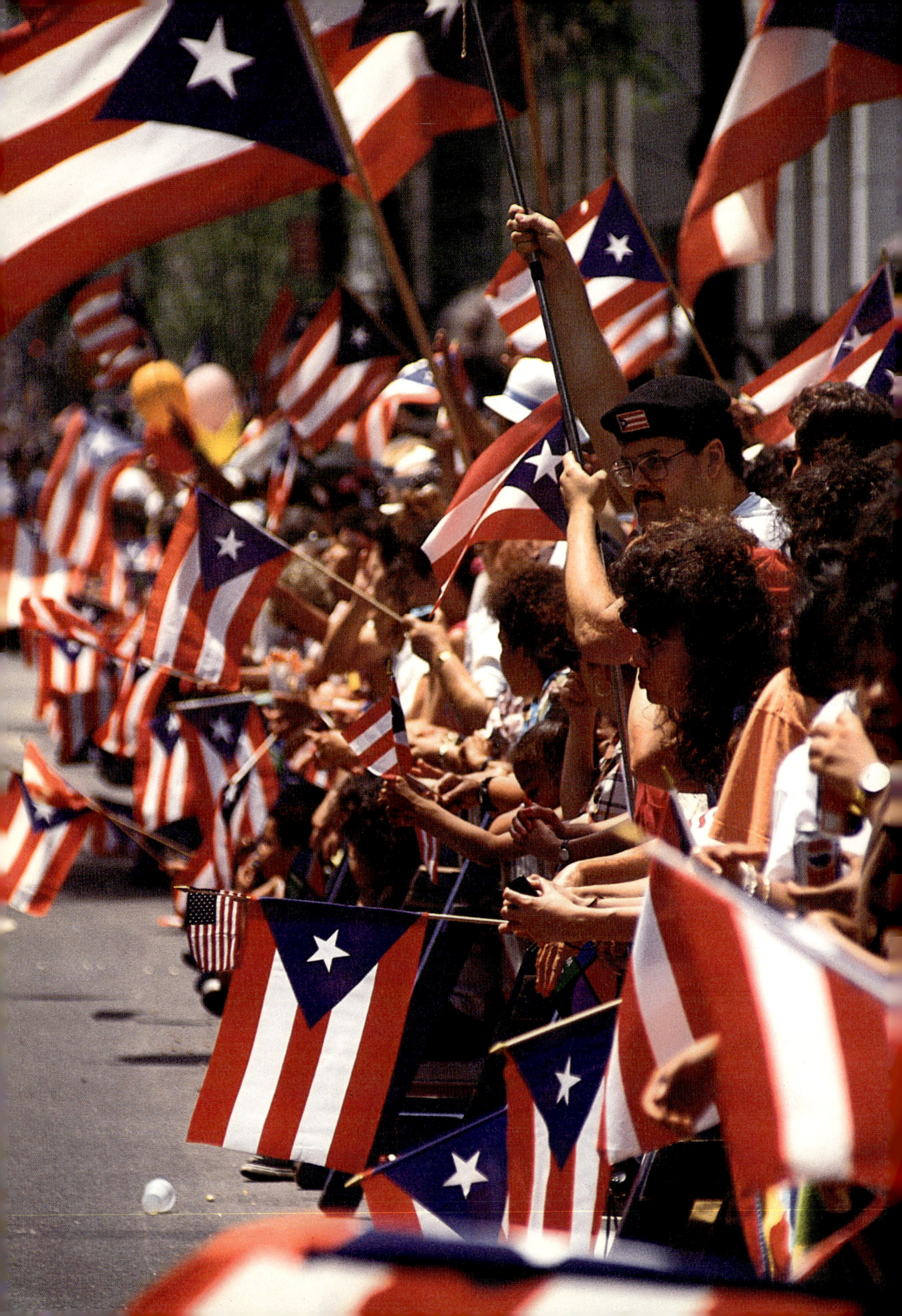

Calendar of Latino Holidays and Celebrations

January 1	Independence Day—Cuba
January 6	Day of the Three Kings
February 2	Day of the Virgin of Candelaria
February 27	Independence Day—Dominican Republic
February or March	Charro Days, Brownsville, Texas
February–March	Carnaval Miami
March 19	Day of Saint Joseph
April 1	PochoFest, Los Angeles
First Saturday after Easter	Hispanic Heritage Festival, Rock Springs, Wyoming
Last week of April	Tucson International Mariachi Conference
May 3	Day of the Holy Cross
May 5	Cinco de Mayo—Mexico
May 14–15	Independence Days—Paraguay
Mid-May	Tejano Conjunto Festival
May 25	Independence Day—Argentina
Early June	Corpus Christi Day
Mid-June	Carnaval Latino of New Orleans
June 24	Day of Saint John the Baptist
July 5	Independence Day—Venezuela
July 20	Independence Day—Colombia
Third week of July	Latino World Festival, Detroit, Michigan
July 28	Independence Day—Peru
Late July	Festival Latino, Washington, D.C.
August 6	Independence Day—Bolivia
August 10	Independence Day—Ecuador

August 16	Restoration Day—Dominican Republic
August 25	Independence Day—Uruguay
Last week of August	Festival del Barrio, Philadelphia
September	Hispanic Heritage Month, Washington, D.C.
Labor Day weekend	Fiesta de las Flores, El Paso, Texas
September 8	Day of Our Lady of Monserratt
September 15	Independence Day—Guatemala, Honduras, Nicaragua, El Salvador, and Costa Rica
September 15-16	Dieciséis (Independence Day)—Mexico
September 18	Independence Day—Chile
September 24	Grito de Lares—Puerto Rico (rebellion against Spanish rule)
Last week of September	Puerto Rican Week Festival, Philadelphia
Last weekend of September	Bayfest, Corpus Christi, Texas
October	Hispanic Heritage Festival, Dade County, Florida
Early October	Border Folk Festival, El Paso, Texas
October 4	Day of Saint Francis
October 12	Día de la Raza/Día de la Hispanidad/ Columbus Day
November 2	Day of the Dead
November 3	Independence Day—Panama
November 19	Discovery Day—Puerto Rico
December 12	Day of Our Lady of Guadalupe
December 16-24	Las Posadas
December 24	Christmas Eve (Nochebuena)
December 25	Christmas Day (Navidad)

Glossary

arepa (ah-RAY-pah): A type of bread made with cornmeal, oil, and sometimes white cheese.

cascarón (cahs-cah-ROHN): A hollow eggshell filled with confetti.

chambelán (cham-bay-LAHN): A boy attendant at a quinceañera.

charreada (chah-rray-AH-dah): A Mexican rodeo.

charro (CHAH-rroh): a Spanish word meaning loud or flashy.

conjunto (cohn-HOON-toh): A Mexican or Texan musical group using accordions, string instruments, and drums.

criollo (cree-OH-yoh): A person of Spanish background born in the Americas.

dama (DAH-mah): A girl attendant at a quinceañera.

Eucharist: The celebration of the death of Jesus Christ through the eating of bread and drinking of wine; also known as Communion.

la misa del gallo (lah MEE-sah dell GAH-yoh): "The Rooster Mass"; the Spanish name for a special Christmas Eve mass held in Catholic churches.

madrina (mah-DREE-nah): A person's godmother.

mariachi (mah-ree-AH-chee): A Mexican musical group using string and brass instruments.

merengue (meh-REN-gay): A Dominican style of dance and music.

padrino (pah-DREE-noh): A person's godfather.

pan de muerto (pahn day MWER-toh): A type of bread baked in a skull shape for Día de los Muertos.

pan dulce (pahn DOOL-say): A type of sweet bread.

pastel (pahs-TEL): A small meat or fish pie.

patron saint: A saint who is believed to protect a certain country or group of people.

peninsular (peh-neen-soo-LAHR): A Spanish-born person living in the Americas in colonial days.

piñata (peen-YAH-tah): A clay or papier-mâché figure filled with candy.

plantain: A variety of banana, used for cooking.

quinceañera (keen-say-an-YAY-rah): A special celebration of a girl's fifteenth birthday.

saint: A historical figure who was believed to perform miracles and show special holiness.

salsa (SAHL-sah): A type of hot sauce; also, a lively style of music.

sancocho (sahn-COH-cho): A soup or stew made of plantains, vegetables, and chicken or beef.

serape (say-RAH-pay): A Mexican poncho or cloak.

shrine: A place set aside to honor God or a saint.

tamales (tah-MAHL-ays): Meat rolled in cornmeal dough, then wrapped in cornhusks or banana leaves and steamed.

turrones (too-RROH-nehs): A type of candy from Spain that is popular in Cuba.

More About Latino Holidays and Celebrations

Catalano, Julie. *The Mexican Americans*. New York: Chelsea House, 1988.

Fagg, John Edwin. *Cuba, Haiti, and the Dominican Republic*. Englewood Cliffs, N.J.: Prentice-Hall, 1965.

Hewett, Joan. *Hector Lives in the United States Now: The Story of a Mexican-American Child*. New York: Lippincott, 1990.

Krull, Kathleen. *The Other Side: How Kids Live in a California Latino Neighborhood*. New York: Lodestar Books, 1994.

Lankford, Mary D. *Quinceañera: A Latina's Journey to Womanhood*. Brookfield, Conn.: Millbrook Press, 1994.

Lansing, Marion F. *Liberators and Heroes of the West Indian Islands*. Boston: L. C. Page, 1953.

Mendez, Adriana. *The Cubans in America*. Minneapolis: Lerner Publications, 1994.

Perl, Lila. *Piñatas and Paper Flowers: Holidays of the Americas in Spanish and English*. New York: Clarion Books, 1983.

Prago, Albert. *The Revolutions in Spanish America: The Independence Movements of 1808-1825*. New York: Macmillan, 1970.

Silverthorne, Elizabeth. *Fiesta! Mexico's Great Celebrations*. Brookfield, Conn.: Millbrook Press, 1992.

Westridge Young Writers Workshop. *Kids Explore America's Hispanic Heritage*. Santa Fe, N.Mex.: J. Muir Publications, 1992.

INDEX

Arepas 9

Baptism 6-8
Bayfest 39
Birthdays 8-12
Border Folk Festival 39

Calle Ocho 32
Carnaval Latino of New Orleans 35
Carnaval Miami 32
Cascarones 16
Catholic church 6, 13-20
Chambelanes 10
Charreada 34
Charro Days 32
Christmas 13-16
Christmas Eve 14
Cinco de Mayo 24-27
Communion. *See* First Communion
Conjunto musicians 35
Criollos 22
Cuban and Cuban American holidays 27-29, 32

Damas 10
Día de la Raza 27
Día de los Muertos (Day of the Dead) 16
Día de los Tres Reyes Magos (Day of the Three Kings) 14
Dieciséis de Septiembre 21-23

Easter 16

Festival del Barrio 36
Festival Latino 36
Fiesta de las Flores 36
Fiestas 6
First Communion 8

Garibaldi Fiesta 34
Good Friday 16
Grito de Dolores 23

Hidalgo, Father Miguel 22
Hispanic American Festival 36
Hispanic Heritage Festival 34, 40
Hispanic Heritage Week 39
Holy Week 16

Independence Day (Central American nations) 23, 30-31
Independence Day (Cuba) 28-31
Independence Day (Mexico) 21-23, 30-31
Independence Day (Puerto Rico) 30-31
Independence Day (South American Nations) 30-31

La misa del gallo 14
Las Posadas 13
Latino World Festival 36
Little Havana 32

Mariachis 34
Martí, José 27-28
Mass 11, 14
Merengue 8

Mexican and Mexican American holidays   21-27, 32-35, 39

Navidad   13-16
New Orleans Hispanic Heritage Foundation   35
Nochebuena   14

Our Lady of Charity's Day   20
Our Lady of Guadalupe   18

Padrinos   7-8, 10
Palm Sunday   16
Pan dulce   13
Pasteles   9, 14
Patriotic holidays   21-29
Patron saints   18
Peninsulares   22
Piñata   9
PochoFest   34
Pochos   34

Puerto Rican holidays   19, 27, 36-39
Puerto Rican Week Festival   39

Quinceañera   10-11

Religious holidays   6-10, 13-20
Rodeo   34

Saint John the Baptist's Day   19
Saints' days   10, 18
Salsa   8
Sancocho   9
Semana Santa   16

Tamales   8
Tejano Conjunto Festival   35
Tucson International Mariachi Conference   34
Turrones   14